CURVEBALLS

poems by

Jo Ann Smith

Finishing Line Press
Georgetown, Kentucky

CURVEBALLS

*To Gale for her relentless encouragement. She brings
rhythm to my blues, meaning to my journey, courage to my voice.*

ACKNOWLEDGMENTS

I wish to thank the Redwood Writers Club anthology publications, Reverberations
I, II, III published by The Sebastopol Center for the Arts and Phoebemd/
Health+Inspiration publication (https://phoebemd.com/emergency-poem-by-jo-
ann-smith) where the following poems have appeared in various versions:

"Purpose Exposed " in *Reverberations III*
"Open" "Unmoored" "My Gilded Pony" in *Phases*
"Emergency" "The Only Girl" "I Never Saw It Coming" in *Crossroads*
"The Bearded Mans Wife" in *Reverberations I*; \ "DragonMoon" "Culling the Herd"
"Beauty and Legend" in *Beyond Distance*
2020 "Life Throws Curveballs" "Under A Blanket of Dark" in . . . And Yet
2019 Redwood Writers Anthology Award of Merit Poet; "Were They Singing" "The
Bearded Man's Wife" "Again" "B'ashert" in *Crow*

Enduring gratitude to my sister poets in the Blue Moon writing group and especially
to our mentors Fran Claggett Holland and Les Bernstein, each a unique and
extraordinary poet. Their counsel and generosity cannot be overstated and will never
be forgotten.

Publisher: Leah Huete de Maines
Editor: Christen Kincaid
Cover Art: Public Domain
Author Photo: Gale Kissin
Cover Design: Elsa Garcia

Order online: www.finishinglinepress.com
also available on amazon.com

Author inquiries and mail orders:
Finishing Line Press
PO Box 1626
Georgetown, Kentucky 40324
USA

Contents

Life Throws Curveballs

it's not always a walk in the park
or fat fastballs down the middle
sometimes life throws curveballs
with a crooked bead on your heart
knocks you off balance, unexpected

a deceptively spun elliptical orb
outwits with an advance smooth and slow
before it dives down rapidly
as it approaches the plate and
drops into the strike zone like a bomb

holding its place as intelligent idiom
this dark art pitch separates
the mimic from the eminent
the good from the great
the ready or not

step up to the plate
measure the speed, read the spin
quiet the din of the crowd
you knew it would come, the veer and vex
of a cleverly bent ball closing in on your
make or break bulwark of readiness

A Crooked Tree

it is all about the root
how nourished
where planted
isolated or conjoined

outside my bedroom window
a crooked tree grew up with me
destined never to grow straight
I was drawn to its nonconformity
as I am drawn to crooked people

who have lived
an examined complicated life
developed a deep root system
to forestall forces
meant to knock them down

who laugh from their bellies
cry when felt tears matter
their powerful
yet fragile humanity
always on display

Hybrid

I am from the fire and water
of mismatched people
parents too young to teach me
what they never knew

I am from dark red wine
and warm flat Guinness
from oppositional cultures
as different as curiosity is to sleep
one as proper as a waltz
the other a wild tarantella

I drink Rosé and cold brews
sleep well and wake up
unencumbered
a hybrid of their union
in a culture of my own
moving in time to the music

The Only Girl

it was always hot on game day
the soft dust around first base
blew like powder in the Santa Ana winds
I was fourteen and knew everything
there was to know about softball

after the fried chicken
corn on the cob
potato salad and chocolate cake
the women would clear and clean
while the rest of us headed to the field

the guys would choose teams
I was the only girl they'd let play
maybe I was the only girl
who wanted to play
either way I had to be in the game

I remember how the leather mitt felt
when I slapped my fist into it
snug and warm on my left hand
soft and pliable from the oil massage
carefully applied the night before

I knew how to play the game
when to play in for a bunt
or back for a double play
how to put my heel on the inside corner
of the bag and stretch to catch the ball
even when to call the infield fly rule

sometimes moving with
the grace of a toreador, fearless
as those grown men ran down the line at me
and the ball smacked my glove
before they flew past

I can still feel the sweat
in my breasts and in my hair
down my back and legs
preparing without knowing for the
big league games to come in my life

Asylum

the black spindly spider
slipping hopelessly down the
stainless-steel sides of the kitchen sink
just to start an ascent again
deserved salvation

I gingerly placed a glass over her
slid a sturdy paper rescue raft
under her exhausted body
carried her to asylum in the garden

it took such little time

why doesn't the almighty
who must see our fragility
how we flail and fail to rescue ourselves
put a bubble around us all
place us back in the garden again

Artistic Aspirations

I am called vengeful merciful almighty
and periodically (think spectacular sunset)
I am an artist inspired
by the spectrum of my own rainbow
to create another masterpiece

on an empty canvas, I painted
with broad strokes
a generous garden
meadows of roses
groves of apples
fields of yellow mustard

it was a terrible mistake
to add that fateful snake—
up against his distemper
my people are cast fallen
god-forbid, I never meant
for them to look so guilty

dissatisfied, I painted them again
in various shades of
black red yellow brown white
seeking more vibrant hues
to rescue my idyllic creation
all to no avail

I shudder today at the chaos on my canvas
images emerge alien to my vision
shall I push the red button
and start all over again
or leave them to their destiny
and concentrate on sunsets

Polaris

on a cloudless night
into the north window of my room
Polaris blinks from its sentinel post
in the black vault of sky
on the edge of the Milky Way

it expects to shine forever
perched above us like the hub of a wheel
neither rises nor sets, appears to stay put
a symbol of constancy while our planet spins
to raise the sun and light the moon

Polaris circles every day discreetly around the pole
a multi-millennial journey begun
five thousand years ago when
pyramids rose from the sands of Egypt
its True North destination
still centuries away

what is true in the heavens
is true in my journey
an internal True North
pulls me like a magnet
offers acumen for lines to cross
roads to take at thresholds of dilemma

a force to keep from
living upside down like a sleeping bat
with no mind for tomorrow
blinded by eclipses of consumption or apathy
numb through the death of verdant Earth

twelve thousand years hence
in a race to reign in our celestial sky
a new star, Vega, a blue-white brighter star
will take her place as steadfast guide
hasten, hasten future star
before it is too late

Under A Blanket of Dark

the colors in my room are black and
infinite shades of gray
breached only by a dot of light
green—from the unseen cable box

sleepless, I imagine
the faint outline of the overhead fan
could be the descent
of an apocalyptic demon
the awful shadow of some sinister power
seen and gone and seen again

balanced on the precipice of a familiar fall
my eyes shut tight against such apparitions
I seek asylum in the company of a
faint hum from a source of power
coyote calls from far away
part of a nocturnal choir in recurrent verse
the wind blows—just enough
to usher jasmine through my open window

blind bewildered moths
compelled by the dark
to forego their frantic
frenzy toward light
are quietly grounded on the walls
at rest in the welcome darkness

in symbiotic harmony
on my side of the world
the earth obscures the sun tonight
leaving the moon turned off
at rest in a dark night sky

securely wrapped
in a blanket of night
enlightened and calmed
by moth and moon
my breath part of a shadow symphony
I am at rest in the paradoxical dark

Look Until You Really See

Sunday morning on the patio at Lowell's
about to dip my buttered toast into an egg
sunny side up when my breakfast mates
see you fly in, land on a wobbly
branch of a young maple tree
and drop the slightest twig into the leaves

Look, she's building a nest!
they watched you
leave and return
leave and return
each time pausing to marvel
as the tiny cradle grew

I never saw you
you were too small for my dimmed eyes
to find in the foliage—I imagined you of course
my mind's eye retained the precision
of your delicate deliberate flight
your in-air suspension

I longed for yesterday's birds' eye vision
lamented the degenerate
blurred obscurity of shapes
the solid things of the outer world
faded, forcing me to look within
and redefine how I see

I Never Saw It Coming

my eyes
wordless interpreters of intimacy
once measured the shape of light and dark
offered insight to my being

they dart now like hummingbirds
their camera-like features
snap pictures of what
will become memory

when I no longer see stars in a star-filled sky
when colors blend to blur
and magical fire offers nothing
but burn and smoke

when all that was sharp loses its edge
and I can't see your eyes gaze into mine
or the contortion of my own tear-stained face
secluded in an immutable night

I can't help it, I think of my mom
whose grip on me was always too tight
and wish for just a moment
to cry upon her shoulder

Beauty and Legend

settled on a rock
overlooking the Pacific Ocean
I track an Orca whale
herself tracking a trail of stars
from Alaska's Bering and Chukchi seas
to the intimate lagoons of Mexico

she moves with the soft roll of summer waves
her grace at sea belies her heaviness
she is no burden to herself

like gods, her kind rise out of the water
to blow their mammal breath
and as a relic of our connection
draw in the air we both need to breathe

I watch her breach, reach for sky
her beauty undiminished by gray patches
and white mottling on her dark skin
encrusted barnacles, ghostly lichen
free ride on her massive back

her black orb eyes are enormous
a deep slow hum, her song
vibrates through sinew and bone
part of a mystical aquatic choir
retelling the history of the world

Culling the Herd

Until the hunted tells her side of the story, the tale of the hunt will always glorify the hunter.
     —paraphrased African proverb

she was not the first to raise her head
freeze in anticipation and bolt
for the camouflage of higher grass
the exquisite senses of her prime
had receded over time

with no more than unabated
flies to disturb her lull
it took her just a second longer
to stop grazing in the lush grasslands
a second, all the time needed
to leave her behind at the back of the herd
aware it was she the cheetah had chosen to cull

pain in her chest grew more insistent as she
labored with animal urgency for breath
her heart pounding, brain scrambled
eyes bright hollows of madness
her cry a shrill mournful horn

she felt the cheetah close in
as the herd pulled away
her mind and body zigzagging
her marauder matching each maneuver
she called on the immortal spirit alive in her core
the summon all strength and will
the plea a hunger to survive

like the murmur of a weakened wind
a sudden stillness sheltered the valley
the lone young cheetah
panting under protruding bones
his paws burning from the chase, gave up
he would go hungry again tonight

his prey, masked in the mystery and magic
of survival, flew as if on wings back to the herd
she was not the fittest, she was not the fastest
but she would not be called nor culled today

Scotch and Sun

drinking a single malt scotch
on a wood planked California deck
each small sip of the golden elixir
smoother than the one before
one large square ice cube afloat in the swirl

watching a tranquil ocean
drenched in the color of Curaçao blue
as it swallowed the golden sun
almost whole in one large gulp

then the remainder
slowly, sip by sip
until the liquid fire slipped entirely
into the belly of a thirsty sea

the horizon abruptly straight-lined
save a scatter of witnessing silver clouds
the bottom of my glass, empty
save a tiny square of melting ice

Again

persimmons are coming again
the wind is holding its breath
ready to blow the leaves off the tree
to expose bejeweled bulbs on craggy limbs
an oddly beautiful barren display

such a reliable tree
noting how swiftly seasons pass
summer yields to fall's festival of growth
fall to its bounty of cold sweet fruit
quiescent winter to embryo buds

and I
having lived another year
even faster than the one before
stop to notice
persimmons are coming again

Unmoored

today's daylight wind, clocked for its
uncommon speed, blew into my mind
with intermittent fury and parboil simmer
fierce then still, sparked then void
like an old battery firing, but
unable to hold a charge

tossed unmoored in this
gale of knockdown force
building up, bowing down
bounced back and forth in an
unrelenting pattern, leaving
only seconds in an untimed pause

a pause
as faint as an echo
no longer than a sigh
yet long enough to choose
to see windswept trash
or listen for answers in the wind

Gilded Pony

I am wide awake
behind closed eyes
in a dream state
afloat on a cloud
holding no rain
detached from a
gorged world
determined to
devour itself

far away I hear
a calliope
I think it is
the 4th of July
and I am ten again
inside a rhythm of
hypnotic carousel spin
holding no reins
my gilded pony strains
to pull each down to up

a euphoric moment
of stunning clarity
more transcendent
than aware
immune to the
passing of time
over before indelible
remembered only for
the longing of its return

On a Leash Free Beach

the dogs are on the loose
beside themselves with
water seaweed each other
nobody is on a leash at this beach
all of us released from
kennels cubicles circumstances
free to flirt with foamy waves
fathom how far the horizon's unbent line
divides sapphire water from opal sky

a multicolored parachute
afloat on bamboo poles
creates a shaded shelter
warm sand runs through my fingers
like the granules of time
my eyes half closed to cloud
the brilliance of this cloudless day
my senses open to the
bliss embodied in this harbor

at home tonight exhausted
the dogs will dream of flying in midair
pirouettes and catching the ball every time
and I, in a dream state of my own
knowing such times last only moments
rarely hours, never years
will hold the treasured time
like a rare bottled missive
before its journey back to sea

The Human Condition

Bodhi is asleep
her black poodle hair
renders her almost invisible
against the sofa's black nubby fabric
if she is dreaming at all
her dreams are not complicated
she will not wake up conflicted
to consider the dream's meaning
her living conditions
unconditionally granted
are blissfully unconsidered
there is no canine condition

but I, diagnosed at birth
with the human condition
am destined to rarely
have a quiet mind
I will know I am
therefore, I will think and
learn that thinking
is burdened with controversy
thought gets caught
in a wicket of ideas
ideas are constrained
curbed by conditions
without which I will not be loved

Bodhi is awake now
staring at me with her grateful eyes
her expression of unconditional love
far more evolved than my own
waiting for me to make the next move
with nothing more on her mind
than what's on mine

Open

consider things that open
jars windows
lights roads
elevators
wounds

clouds open for rain
doors to neighbors
strangers and trick or treaters
minds to wisdom
hearts to love

contemplate the pill bug
a roly-poly creature
its back crinkled like a lobster tail
touch it and afraid, it rolls into a ball
undaunted and curious, it opens
like an unclenched fist

Emergency

never a place one wants to be, especially alone
in a hurry they weigh me, no time to remove
shoes extra layers glasses ring watch, annoyed
my weight will be inflated
wheeled to a small sterile space, single bed, medical
charts thumbtacked in random order to lime green walls
I respond to the instruction *you can lie down now*
an air conditioner blows cold, my breath is labored and shallow
an invisible pressure on my chest more terrifying than pain

blood pressure high, oxygen low
scar on my left breast placid but ever present
a masked nurse, I can only see her eyes
knocks, but does not wait for an answer
pushes a lab cart through the door
I tell her I'm a 'tough stick' ask if she's the 'A Team'
she may have smiled, but she pokes a needle
and misses a vein three times—once in my helpless
bloodless hand—before the A team arrives

blood finally flowing I ask for a blanket and am told
I've put the gown on backward
it should open in the back, that's why you're cold
embarrassed, I wonder if they flaunt this knowledge
as a trade-off for kindness
one leaves, another arrives pushing a different cart
complete with tv screen displaying blue blips
and grainy green graphics, a re-run loop of my heart
the antenna stuck to pivotal parts of my chest, I think
how convenient for me to have put the gown on backwards

more tests, some repeated, but mostly waiting
for another knock that ignores an invitation
my mind keeps bargaining
that my life has been rich and if this is the end, so be it
but I am terrified, not ready, too much to repair
happenings not to be missed, a heart not fully opened

tears roll into my mask, I can't pray
it seems so selfish to add one more plea
when God is clearly not coping

after six cold hours I am discharged
poked prodded scanned
they think they know what it isn't
your doctor will call you, one more test
and we think we'll know what it is

DragonMoon

born in the Year of the Dragon
your eyes like the first rays of dawn
your spirit royal blue as the edge of flame
brilliant bold benevolent
never Job's fire-breathing beast
nor prey for dragon-slaying knights
   more Puff than pugilist

born a Cancer Moon Child
drawn to the dark side
through cycles that ebb and flow
in and out of light and dark
I shift shape lunar-like
reliant on sun for light
illuminated by your lustre

separately connected you and I
by myth and magic
staples of fable and legend
the majesty of dragons
the mystery of moons

here in our earthly garden
grasses wax and wane and waltz in the wind
soft petaled roses bloom under the pelting
of a hard-shelled walnut tree
and I swing through the air
over the moon
in a hammock of dragon mettle

when the orb of night is full
coyotes howl in the canyon
our shadows fall long across the yard
we are suspended in silence
enthralled and bewitched

moonlight reveals sundial
pathways to new garden vistas
to Gracie's grave under the encroaching oak
and to the front door of our cave
where dragons go to rest
and the moon shines through the rooftop cupola

She Brings Rhythm to My Blues

she is dazzling
as a fireworks finale and
as light draws even a blind moth
I am drawn to her mystery

her intoxicating embodiment
of music love and freedom
once believed beyond my reach
flood my senses

the deluge finds its way to river
a fog of foregone destiny lifts and
the haunt of the past begins to vanish
as a nightmare left behind at dawn

we remain as different as melody from verse
yet harmonious as a rainbow's striations
she is the poignant passion in a minor chord
she brings rhythm to my blues

B'ashert
(Yiddish for that which is meant to be)

there you are alone
still on the water
a ghostly apparition
barely causing a ripple
my breath quickens
I lament your isolation

a white pelican
among drab brown minions
were you exiled
not a bird of their feathers
did your coat of no color
cast you out alone
no kindred companion
no lover of your own

wait, they're coming!
a flock of brown feathered pelicans
surround you on the feeding ground
in their midst another white pelican
she alights beside you
your great wings lift to receive her

after the clamor of splash and feed
your consort at your side soaring
I watch the flock follow you
deeper into the inlet until
I can no longer distinguish
you from them

from the fortune of this witness
the virtue of this moment
comes an inhale of awareness
a mystery of destiny

when someone rare finds
another's life to share
scarcity yields to b'ashert—
that which is meant to be

An Argument

slog with me
through the heavy wet grass
past the weeping trees
over the moss slicked rocks
to the edge of the cliff

a crosswise torrent
threatens our balance
weighed-down birds, their wings
blown from under them
flail to stay aloft

clasp my hand
be steady with me on the cliff
find the north star
summon its renouncement
of doubt

we have been here before
and will be again, even so
recall how brightly
we shine in the sun

Addiction

how can I help you
I'm on a diet
I'll just have the apple/cranberry salad
with balsamic on the side
and a diet Coke

I succumbed to the soothing seduction of sugar
to supplant the bitter taste of mother's milk
taunting memories still trigger
compulsive stuffing to fill
some early unexamined emptiness

how was your lunch
would you like to see the dessert menu
it won't hurt to look

satiation speaks with a forked tongue
obliterates the distinction
between want and need
sets off hunger sirens
when there is no emergency

convinces me it is too late
to ever be what I might have been
declares my character weak
whispers obsessive heavy thoughts
about willpower and weight

murmurs soft deceitful wicked words
deadbolts to lock in cravings, shame
from which even a necklace of garlic
is no protection

see something you like
you have flourless chocolate cake
we do!

I can't pass that up
and a scoop of vanilla ice cream
on the side

Matriarch

"*Swallow it!*" she ordered
as the acrid taste of the slimy greens
she pulled like weeds from our back yard
began to overtake the rebelling buds in my mouth

I tried to imagine
my grandma's flour dusted hands
kneading a bread loaf into shape
or pulling pasta into precisely sculpted gnocchi
to bubble softly in sweet homemade sauce
and couple with pungent parmesan

but no culinary fantasy could stop
the backward revulsion of my gut
to these repulsive greens

I held the bite, lips pursed tight
gathering courage to not
throw up the foul offensive food
and then I swallowed

she would squeeze my cheek
too hard sometimes
and say in her lyrical native tongue
"*que bella faccia*"

her eyes green shades
of the greens she grew
her skin smooth as a castelvetrano
her hair piled loosely atop her head
auburn and gray strands
escaping to frame my memory
"*what a beautiful face*"

the respect I came to have for her
a widowed immigrant matriarch
a powerful woman against whose body
I measured my growth would not be real to me

or matter in my life until long after she died
but to this day I will not eat zucchini
and just the sight of boiled greens
puts my stomach on alert

Those Bus Riding Goldfish

I thought if I heard my mother
tell that goldfish story one more time
I'd go belly up myself
you'd think it was some extraordinary effort
to carry home a Chinese food carton
to transport two goldfish while she held on
to the upper bar on a bumpy bus

I never believed she didn't have a seat—
convinced she made that up
to embellish the story and stories like that
all intended to imprint on my pliable nature
how much she sacrificed and
what she expected in return

maybe it was more difficult than I know
to keep her balance on those bumpy old buses
maybe those goldfish hit their little orange heads
on top of that carton and water sloshed
through the cracks onto unforgiving passengers
every time the bus lunged
if nobody offered her a seat and she stood that way
purse in one hand goldfish in the other—
I shouldn't minimize the sacrifice

but through the years
I felt a wave of motion sickness
when she talked about those bus riding goldfish
I can't remember a goldfish bowl at home
I don't recall feeding or caring about any goldfish
when I see goldfish in aquariums today
I feel ungrateful for how hard it must have been

years later, shortly before she died, she called to ask
How's your writing going?
Don't look for me to be on the best seller list anytime soon

I don't know about that; I know you could be
I love you mom
I love you more
hanging up I sighed and slumped in one motion
no wonder I feel guilty all the time

The Bearded Man's Wife
(ekphrastic poem based on Picasso Vase, edition 500)

if I gazed at your face
five hundred times
I might not see the mystery there
or would I

the irregular glaze of your face, stained perhaps by tears
like the one about to fall from your eye
bears no resemblance
to your more vivid mate
the eponymous Bearded Man
his masculine face a rich smooth bronze
expressive, decidedly dominant

your hair hangs loosely on the left
tightly braided on the right
held back with adorning
ribbons and bows, a whimsical leaning?
yet how to know your nature
whether carefree or contained

who were you
why is your face
frozen in anonymity
were you a woman of substance
a vessel of life, more than
the Bearded Man's Wife

the multidimensional ewer of you
the curves and dips and depths
of the white earthen clay
reveal as a flat, plain mask
your eyes, if not frightened, lack passion
as if they see nothing
as if you were to yourself invisible

I could see your face five hundred times more
to explore what Picasso ignored
a plainly exposed misogynist
he captured your beauty; it was all that he saw
whether lapse or intention
your dimension was sadly dismissed
you should have been painted with awe

29

Purpose Exposed

Ekphrastic Poem
Photograph by Ruth Bernhard, Two Leaves, 1952

with the surety of its eye this camera
caught us just so, perfectly posed
exposed in new light
two leaves on sturdy stalks
life support to flowers we lift up in glory

introverts to their
floral extravagance
our presence ignored or unseen
in the blaze of their exhibition
yet our purpose is undeterred

transfixed by colorless fusion
of black and gray with
tones of umber turning
no rose or lilac to detract
from the ritual of our opening and closing

younger sister, the fiber of our eco-system
runs through your unveiled veins
pulses a continuity of growth
while my receding unmapped tributaries
hold the consciousness of fulfilled purpose

the tender modesty of your unfurling
like a ballerina's first dance, hesitant
and unstoppable, shy yet determined
poised for its intimate destiny
in the cycle of renewal

holding nothing back we are
breathtaking in this green-less light
in our after-five attire
cloaked in royal shades of fade to black
captured in a flash

Boxed-In

stored in the barn
hauled from place to place
old containers I don't bother to open
some with labeled memories I want to forget

it is a massive barn
a depository for trash and treasure
hidden away, misplaced
rarely subject to my own review

I rearrange the clutter from time to time
hide certain boxes in dark abandoned stalls
believing out of sight might mean
they are not here at all

a thousand photos chronicling my life
are stored in the loft
pictures meant to be passed on
to kin who barely knew me

dim light in the barn
filters through dirt-streaked windows
turns shadows into images
imagination into fear of what might be lurking

stairs with audible moans threaten to let go
loose boards bow free of rusty nails
thick helter-skelter webs hang high in the rafters
launch pads for spider trapezists

then, without warning, the musty barn burned to the ground
boxes of the past blew away in the smoke
to reveal an open expanse of heaven
dominated by a singular moon
unabashedly full of itself

under the canopy of a million celestial miracles
in the presence of a force so strong it pulls tides off the shore
and sends them back again and again with rhythmic certainty
my jaw hung ajar in awe
the fulness of the moon commands the night
its discovery revealed by loss of what was never mine

Purple Dust

sometimes I pray
not knowing if prayers
are anything more than a sigh
carried by the wind into nothing

I have felt an untold presence
but don't believe it's real
I have gathered at the river
never witnessed angels dancing
worshiped at the mountain
never to reach higher ground

so done am I
with this twist of ambivalence
my own tapestry
of rainbow-colored silk
adrift, unspooled

so tired am I
with this travel back and forth
on tumbledown terrain
across a bridge of my own mistakes
to find the river Jordan
with its promise of deliverance
from this blur of purple dust

before my life is over
will some omniscient narrator
whose eyes see light and dark
in their original colors
reveal the mysteries of life
before, now and after

or will it be enough, may I be content
to cultivate a heart that beats
in rhythm with a universal pulse
and keep a steady grip
on the edge of this ancient rock
until with wonder I let it go

Were They Singing

were they
singing praying daydreaming
was the Rabbi droning on
maybe they were sleeping
I used to fall asleep in church

the embrace of shabes peace
brought them to the shul that day
where unsuspected terror struck

senseless serial assaults
spike my blood pressure
even evoke a momentary outrage
then fade
often before the next news cycle begins

this one
threatens my balance
spinning dizzy falling
on my knees immobile
stuck in centuries old tear soaked mud
not ready to resurrect

what is this sorrow
I am not a Jew
what is this compulsion to
tightly hold this pain
as if letting go would shatter a trust
but with whom

tomorrow
time
the grand arbiter
may work its magic
begin to crowd out
yesterday's biddings

but today
aware the sound of breaking glass
has never cost me more than
just an inconvenience
today
eighty years since Kristallnacht
today I am a Jew

Write It All Down

here's the thing about a poet's heart
you can put it in a vise
and squeeze it
to its last drop of essence
but if you don't kill it
no matter how slowly
it will fill again

it will grapple with the bramble
of necessary contradictions—
compassion or vengeance
curiosity or conviction
equality or submission—
and in an honest quest
for illusive truth
write it all down

poets live on the edge
peer into the abyss
pause, then step back
to secure footing on solid ground
and look up to the grandeur
of the unexplainable
and write it all down

so on one Saturday
my heart was drained by
the inhumanity of humans
and on the next Saturday
in a room filled with the wise
soulful words of poets I love
I believed again

I can hold gnawing disillusionment
in one hand and with the other hand
cradle my heart, take a deep breath
feel the flow of fresh infusion
pulse through my veins
to a heart beaten down, but born to beat on
willing to fill again and compelled
to write it all down

On A Bench

on a bench overlooking an endless lake
a white swan glides on the rippled silver water
three small identicals content
to trail in her gentle wake

sun diamonds bounce around
them like blinking pixel lights
the scene beckons peace, so I sit down
to have a chat with myself
take time to quiet my interrupting mind

conjure the beginning of a conversation
with no contradictions no argument
with my point of view, see if like a Magpie
I might recognize my image
in the watery mirror

Finale

I played softball when I was young
loved the competition
needed to win, hated to lose

I was a catcher
the strategic brain of the team
in a position to see the whole field

now older, the tattoos of becoming
etched on my being
my true identity claimed

I wonder
through it all
who have I become

in the descending bend of my life
before I encounter becomings unknown
or take my place in an eternal void

when the people I love
or love me most
are barely visible in a dividing fog

when earthly matters no longer matter
and I am no longer intrigued
by being a human being becoming

at the end of the game
when I can see the whole field again
I trust I will conjure

a fireworks finale
dazzled by
who I have become

www.ingramcontent.com/pod-product-compliance
Lightning Source LLC
Chambersburg PA
CBHW020220090426

42734CB00008B/1144